The Daemonolater's Guide to

Daemonic Offerings

Ψ

S. Connolly

The Daemonolater's Guide to

Daemonic Offerings

Ψ

S. Connolly

DB PUBLISHING 2015

MMXV

DB Publishing is an arm of Darkerwood Publishing Group, PO Box 2011, Arvada, CO 80001.

ISBN: 978-1512017021

Book Design by Kim Anderson and Stephanie Reisner

For all those who have dedicated themselves to the Daemonic and serve in the temples of the Gods.

Introduction

Offerings have always been a part of Daemonolatry, albeit more subtly. People didn't get hung up on them so much back in my early days of practice like they do now. It was just more widely accepted back then that these things were offerings to the Daemonic. Oleums, incenses, wine, candles, food, and most importantly blood are the standard fare, but before we get into WHAT you can offer a Daemon, let's start with the why. We'll work our way to what, when, and finally how.

Think of this guide as your official introduction to offerings for the Daemonic. Please note that by Daemonic, we mean "Divine Intelligences" which is a general term for many spirit types, including some that some people would consider Gods/Goddesses/Planetary/Elemental/Djinn (i.e. Goetic) etc… Daemon is a VERY broad term. For more information about Daemonolatry, see *The Complete Book of Demonolatry*.

1

Why Would You Make Offerings to Daemons?

Oftentimes people who get into Daemonolatry are surprised when they learn we give the Daemons offerings. Offerings are often seen as some kind of groveling or woo-woo, it seems. On the contrary, offerings are tokens of devotion, or signs of respect, and can be given out of gratitude as well. An offering can be made in exchange for something, too, as in pact making (see the book *Daemonic Pacts*).

When you invite someone into your house – you offer them something to drink, maybe offer them food. Right? Why should this be any different for your Daemonic guests?

You offer them incenses made specifically to please them. This is no different than cooking a low-carb, sugar free meal for a diabetic house guest. You may offer the Daemonic an oleum you've made just for them, too. You may choose candles to use in a color that corresponds to their nature. You might also offer them the ritual wine. Finally – the most common offerings in most Daemonic rituals is blood. Not a lot, just a drop or two taken in the least

2

destructive way possible, usually by diabetic lancet device. Please see the section on blood offerings for more information. These offerings serve to make your Daemonic guests comfortable AND promote a harmonious working relationship.

Some Daemons prefer certain types of offerings. For example, while you could give certain Khemetic Daemons blood, they actually prefer milk and honey, or even wine. Bastet is fond of water. Other Daemons, on the other hand, prefer blood offering, some more than others. Belphegor, Ba'al, and Balberith are three Daemons who tend to prefer blood offering. You can see more about certain Daemonic under types of offerings this booklet.

Types of Offerings

The following are the types of offerings you can leave. It is important to understand that the most appropriate offerings are always "sacrifices" in some way. Basically to sacrifice something doesn't mean to kill it. It simply means to give something (usually something you need) up. When you do that, you make it sacred. This means that even in animal sacrifice, you should ONLY sacrifice animals meant for your food! Remember that you are giving something up.

Blood Offerings

In my book *Keys of Ocat* I explain why Daemonolatry is considered a bloodletting tradition. This particular section, to put it into context, is explaining the various parts of the soul, of which the heart is one. *"The heart, also known as the Ib, is the blood passed on from mother to child. This is why, in Daemonolatry, a magician who gives his blood in offering, even in small amounts, is giving something very sacred of himself. The blood is the life. The life passed from parent to child. Some have argued this actually means DNA. Perhaps, but we won't get into waxing philosophic here. Suffice to say this is, in part, why*

4

Daemonolatry is a blood-letting tradition and why blood is viewed as being so important."

Daemonolaters take blood in the least destructive way possible and one only needs a drop or two. Diabetic lancet devices are great for this. Women can use menstrual blood. You can also use blood from cuts, scrapes, or picked scabs. Could you use a sacrifice like a Chicken? Certainly, however it takes much less courage to sacrifice something from another living thing than it does to sacrifice from the self, so if you are truly dedicated to the spirit you're working with, sacrificing blood to that spirit is not too much to ask.

Of course Daemonolaters have been chastised for this practice by magicians who believe that if you sacrifice blood to a Daemon – the Daemon will demand more and more blood until you either kill yourself or go crazy. This is untrue. I've been working with Daemons for over thirty years now and I have never been asked to kill myself or give more and more blood. The Daemonic knows what's sacred. Giving blood to a Daemon also does not give it control over you. It is still a consensual relationship of give and take. A Daemon can only take over your will if you hand it over.

Blood is an appropriate offering because **it is something you sacrifice of yourself.**

My good friend Angie Anon put it eloquently when she said on a blog on demonolatry.org regarding sacrifice, *"For the spiritual side of things, the sacrifice, which is the act of making something sacred, of a few drops of your own blood as offering to deity is the most personal and highest offering you can give."*

The fact that you were willing to sacrifice a part of yourself to give to the Daemonic speaks highly of your dedication to the Daemon or the magickal operation – or both.

Daemons who prefer Blood Offerings include Ba'al, Balberith, Belphegor, Berith, Babael, and Beelzebub

However, most all Daemons will tolerate blood offerings well except for Khemetic Daemons. It's not that they don't tolerate them more than they just don't seem to care for them one way or the other. The only time this isn't the case is during curses, death rituals, or other *dark* magick.

Wine and Alcohol Offerings

This is actually one of the more common offerings for Daemons. Usually it's the wine from ritual that is either left for the Daemon on the altar, or taken outside and offered as a libation to the Daemonic. The type and quality of the wine doesn't really matter. What matters is that you paid for it with your own earned money, or you made it yourself. There has to be sacrifice to make it sacred and therefore worthy of offering.

Tobacco Offerings

While tobacco isn't often widely used in Daemonic offerings, it is used a great deal in ancestral offerings, unless said ancestor hated tobacco. Don't dismiss tobacco and other like plants as offerings.

Animal Sacrifice/Offering

This is generally reserved for big events, festivals, group rites, or very important work with the Daemonic. The sacrifice should be of a food animal, the animal should be sacrificed humanely, and the flesh later consumed (not burnt offering) at a feast following the rite. Ba'al Rites and the big

Fire Festivals come to mind here as rituals that tend to warrant animal sacrifice. Amducius, Flereous, Sorath, and even Satan seem to appreciate this type of offering. They will also accept animal effigies (i.e. animals made of sticks or paper or some other substance than flesh) burnt on bonfires as a form of burnt offering. It's the effort and thought that counts, so why kill an animal unless you're doing a pig roast and you have humane means to sacrifice a pig?

Plants and Flowers

Those you grow yourself hold more meaning. But certainly the time you spend picking wild flowers will also be appreciated, especially for Daemons like Ashtaroth, Unsere, Leviathan, Lucifer, Asafoetida (considering she's a plant genius/Daemon), Sitri, and Verrier. Daemons with more feminine energy, perhaps even earthy or watery in some way, strongly resonate with plants and plant energy as offerings. Marigolds are common offerings for the Death Daemonic. (See *Honoring Death* and *Keys of Ocat* to learn more about the Death Daemonic.)

Food Offerings

Fruit is a great choice for Daemons like Hecate, Anubis, and Daemons whose purpose it is to transform the living to the dead. There is a life force in fruit that those Daemons seem to enjoy. While it's best if you grow it yourself, you can also buy it. I will often use apples and oranges because they're inexpensive and plentiful in autumn and winter when these particular types of Daemons reign supreme. Dates and figs are also good options.

Milk and Honey is a fantastic offering for Khemetic, Roman, and Green Daemons because it's often more traditional. No one expects you to keep bees or raise cattle or goats for milk, but if you do – more power to you! If you have pets around the house, you might want to keep this offering in a closed room or closed container. Otherwise it won't be the Daemon getting it, it will be the cat (or dog).

Nuts are also a good choice to share with ancient God/Goddess Daemons.

Breads/Cakes are a good overall offering choice for any Daemon. You may even choose to share it with them during ritual. You would eat part of it, and give the rest to them. The Daemons don't mind sharing. If you bake the bread or cakes yourself, all the better.

Sexual Fluid

Most Daemons will accept semen and vaginal lubricant fluid as offerings, but this type of offering works best with Fire Daemons like Asmodeus, Ashtaroth, Amducius, and Focalor.

Candles

Candles are another common offering suitable for the Daemonic Divine.

Incense and Oluems

Homemade loose incenses and self-made oleums are always a good choice for offerings because each mixture will contain plant matter and essences formulated specifically for that Daemon. Yes, you could only use incenses for earth, air, and fire Daemons and Oleum for watery Daemons, but really – all of them will appreciate both.

Creative Offerings

Paintings, Jewelry, Pottery, Textiles, Beaded Jewelry or Charms Etc... Don't forget creative offerings. If you took time to make it, and you put your heart and soul into it, it is suitable as an offering to the Daemonic. So artists rejoice! A beautiful handmade vase filled with cut flowers from your own garden is a better offering than a piece of stale, store-bought bread.

Music, Poetry, and Writing can also be suitable offerings for the Daemonic. If you put work into it, and you can sing, play, compose, recite, or read what you've created during your offering rituals, this is an offering very pleasing to the Daemonic

Creative offerings are most appreciated by Daemons of music, writing, arts, and crafts. Most magick/sorcery Daemons fall into this category including Thoth, Seshat, Hecate, and Delepitoré.

Burnt Offerings

Burnt offerings are usually effigies. Something in the likeness of something else, burnt as representational. However, a burnt offering can also be a written devotional sealed (or not) with a drop of blood, or simply blood itself on a piece of paper, burnt in the flames of the offering bowl. The fire transforms the offering from the physical to the spiritual. Just about anything you can offer can also be burnt as an offering. Though effigies, incense, devotionals, and blood on paper are the most common types of burnt offering you'll see in Daemonolatry. All Daemons will accept burnt offerings.

When to Make Offerings

Offerings can be made during high holy days, specific Daemonic holy days, or really any time you wish. Many Daemonolaters keep at least one or two altars dedicated to specific Daemons within their homes. These altars may also serve as offering altars for those particular Daemons.

In this instance many people will make a daily offerings, or at least weekly offerings to the Daemon. *When* you make your offerings is determined solely by you, and you alone. There is no wrong time of the day to give an offering. However, some people do believe that there are certain demons who prefer offerings by night and others by day. Hecate is a good example of this in that offerings to her are often left under the darkness of night.

If you have an altar to a particular demon within your home chances are you already know, by tradition or instinct, when to leave offerings. If you aren't sure a little research should provide you with an answer.

How to Make Offerings

Some people prefer to leave offerings without much consideration to method. They'll simply walk into the temple, leave the offering, and go about their daily business.

Others prefer formal ritual and deep respect shown through action. You will have to choose what is right for you. In more formal offerings, the offering is carried aloft in front of you to the altar. You would kneel before the altar and hold the offering on high, reciting any prayers or devotionals at that time. The offering would then be placed upon the altar, the dedicant would then bow their head in prayer or moment of silence, and then back away from the altar, head bowed, never turning their back to the altar out of deep respect for the Daemonic force they are offering to.

Admittedly this type of formal offering is not for everyone. Especially those who may not view the Daemonic in *that* way.

Offering Altars

When creating your offering altars it is important to seriously consider everything that goes onto that altar. The first consideration is the type of altar covering or altar cloth. Color is an important factor here and should correspond with the Daemon's preference. Next, altars are often adorned with statues of the Daemon being honored. This may not always be an easy task since not all Daemons have a readily available statuary. For example, when working with Leviathan or Dag on, a statue of a serpent or snake may suffice. Be creative with this. Drawings or artwork of Daemons, or even framed sigils are appropriate for a Daemonic altar on which offerings will be left.

Next, you want to add candles to the altar. Many people prefer the seven-day candles, which you can often find cheaply at most Botanica's or sometimes even grocery stores depending on where you live. Votive in tea light candles are also appropriate as prayer candles. Since altars like this often serve several purposes, such as leaving offerings, for prayer, and is devotional altars for the particular Daemon you're working with. The color of the candles should correspond with the demon. The exception to this for the prayer candles, which should be white. Prayer

12

candles are often lit during prayer and then extinguished afterward, whereas the main altar candles are often burned as offerings to the daemonic, and can be left burning hours at a time. Please note that candles should never be left unattended, especially if you have children or pets in the house. You don't want to burn down your house.

Once these elements have been taking care of you can choose with what else to put on your altar. For example, an altar to Leviathan might include a chalice for leaving wine offerings or offerings of water. If you tend to leave a lot of flower offerings for that particular demon you may include a vase that goes to that daemonic altar. You may have a bowl for fruit offerings or food offerings. Or you may simply have a burning bowl to offer burnt offerings. Some people will leave small finger bowls on altars to collect drops of blood.

Now onto the matter of the size of the altar. These altars can be as small or as large as you want them to be. However, each daemon should have their own altar. This ensures the proper respect is paid to each daemon individually.

Everything you put on your altar needs to be properly cleaned and consecrated to the Daemonic force you're working with. This includes washing each item thoroughly, running it through the smoke of frankincense, and anointing it with an appropriate oleum. The altar itself should be washed with a holy cleansing water. By holy I mean a wash made with frankincense, benzoin, and sage.

The altar should be thoroughly cleaned and re-consecrated once a month. Offerings themselves should be replenished as needed. Or wanted. This means that fresh flowers should be replaced when the flowers are dry. New wine should be added to the chalice when it has evaporated. New water should be added to water bowls or chalices once it has evaporated. More blood should be added when the blood in the bloodletting bowl is dry. Food offerings should be removed and replaced when it either begins to rot or has dried out. Food offerings should never be thrown away, they should be taken to an outdoor offering space and committed to the ground. The same should be done for wines and waters if they have not evaporated. All spent incense and ashes of burnt offerings should also be taken to the outdoor offering space and committed to the ground.

Offering Spaces Outdoors

The outdoor offering space is a sacred space where offerings are left to be committed back to the earth. The space can be as small as a pot of soil on a balcony or porch, or is large as a 9 x 9 room. The size of the space really depends on how much room you have.

You will need to consecrate the space with salt and water, and fumigated with either sage or frankincense. Some people may choose to bury protective witch bottles at the four corners of their consecrated space. Others still may choose to erect natural altars within the outdoor offering space. At least one area of the offering space should include a small hole in circled by rocks. This hole should be the size of your palm. Use the rocks for outdoor bloodletting during Ba'al Rites, or Rites of Belphegore. The hole itself should be used for bloodletting, libations, and offering ashes.

The stones not need to be of a certain type, however if you are doing certain types of magical work you may choose to use corresponding stones, and change them out as needed. I prefer simple River rock, or rocks found during hikes or gardening.

If you are going to leave the remainder of fruit and food offerings outdoors you will need a larger space. Those offering should be left in a pile away from the circle of stones. If you are using pots of soil as your outdoor offering space, keep two. One for your circle of stones, and one for spent food offerings.

If you do it right the outdoor offering space will include a small mulch pile where your spent food offerings are left. If you turn it, you can use it for the garden. The stones should regularly be cleaned and replaced around the offering hole, which may need to be re-dug after time. The outdoor offering space should be kept free of debris and non-spiritual items. Some people may choose to include outdoor statuary in this space. Others have installed Zen rock gardens, meditation spaces, or outdoor artwork to transform their offering space into a welcoming ritual space. All of this is up to you and should reflect you and your spiritual leanings. More personalized the space, the more meaning it will hold for you, and the more sacred it will be made for the spirits that you honor.

Offering Ritual

As I mentioned previously, there are those who like simple ritual and there are those who prefer formal ritual. If you like simple ritual you need but simply carrier offering to the altar, set it upon it, offer a prayer or moment of silence, and then go about your day. However, for those who prefer more formal ritual the following is provided as an outline for you to formulate your own offering rituals.

Begin with the newly consecrated altar to the demon you are leaving offerings for. Prepare yourself by bathing and dressing and ritual attire. For Daemonolaters this would be standard black ritual robes. If you do not have ritual attire you may choose to submit your offering in the nude, or wearing a solid color pleasing to the Daemon.

Collect your offerings and take them to the sacred space within which the altar stands. Approach the altar with love in your heart, and affection toward the Daemonic force you're working with. Like the altar candles and any incense. Poor any water, wine, or alcohol. Then hold your offering on high, recite the Daemonic enn/invocation, and then say:

"Behold *spirit*, it is I, *your name*, dedicated to you, who stands before your altar. I offer unto you this *nature of*

17

offering that it pleases you, and tells you of my undying devotion. Please accept this from my heart."

Place the offering upon the altar. Offer drops of blood if that is your desire. Light a prayer candle and proceed to say any relevant prayers. Spend a few moments in silent reflection, allowing the Daemonic a bathe you in its light. Then stand and extinguish the prayer candle. You may leave the altar candles burning if you will be nearby. If not, extinguish them as well. Then, with head bent in reverence, back out of the room still facing the altar. Never turn your back on the altar as that is akin to shunning the divine.

This concludes the standard offering ritual. Outdoor offerings are conducted in the same way.

It is my hope this booklet has served as an informational guide to the art of daemonic offering. As long as you always give offerings from your heart you can never do it wrong. ~

Additional Resources

Daemonolatry

- *The Complete Book of Demonolatry* Connolly, S.
- *The Daemonolater's Guide to Daemonic Magick* Connolly, S.

Prayer

- *Ater Votum: Daemonolatry Prayer*

Sacred Deamonic Religious Ceremony

- *Abyssal Communion & Rite of Imbibement*

Pact Making

- *Daemonic Pacts* Connolly, S.

NOTES

More from DB Publishing & Official Melissa Press

By S. Connolly

- The Complete Book of Demonolatry
- The Daemonolater's Guide to Daemonic Magick
- The Art of Creative Magick
- Daemonolatry Goetia
- Infernal Colopatiron or Abyssal Angels: Redux
- Curses, Hexes & Crossings: A Magician's Guide to Execration Magick
- Honoring Death: The Arte of Daemonolatry Necromancy
- Necromantic Sacraments
- Kasdeya Rite of Ba'al: Blood Rite of the Fifth Satan
- Nuctemeron Gates
- Abyssal Communion & Rite of Imbibement
- Keys of Ocat
- Drawing Down Belial
- Bound By Blood: Musings of a Daemonolatress

By M. Delaney

- Sanctus Quattuordecim: Daemonolatry Sigil Magick

By E. Purswell

- Goetic Demonolatry

By Martin McGreggor

- Paths to Satan

By Scott Hobbs

- Gates of Lucifer

Various Authors (Compilation Books)

- My Name is Legion: For We Are Many
- Demonolatry Rites
- Ater Votum: Daemonolatry Prayer
- Satanic Clergy Manual

Forthcoming from DB Publishing & Official Melissa:

- Wortcunning for Daemonolatry – S. Connolly
- A Witch's Book of Recipes – Brian McKee
- Grimorium Daemonolatrie – S. Connolly & M. Delaney (Melissa)
- Sacrae Infernales – S. Connolly

Workbooks and Journals by S. Connolly

- The Goetia Workbook
- 30 Days of Spirit Work
- The Spirit Workbook
- The Meditation Journal
- Ritus Record Libri

13399843R00021

Printed in Great Britain
by Amazon.co.uk, Ltd.,
Marston Gate.